Spark

IGNITING YOUR GOD-GIVEN CREATIVITY

April Yamasaki

 MennoMedia

Harrisonburg, Virginia
Kitchener, Ontario

Spark: Igniting Your God-Given Creativity
© 2015 by MennoMedia, Harrisonburg, Virginia 22802.
Released simultaneously in Canada by Faith & Life Resources,
Kitchener, Ontario N2G 3R1.
All rights reserved.
International Standard Book Number: 978-0-8361-9960-4
Printed in the United States of America
Design by Merrill Miller
Cover photo: oksana nazarchuk/Thinkstock

Unless otherwise noted, Scripture text is quoted, with permission, from the *New Revised Standard Version*, © 1989, Division of Christian Education of the National Council of Churches of Christ in the United States of America.

Hymns referenced in this book are from *Hymnal: A Worship Book* (Faith & Life Resources, 1992), *Sing the Journey* (Faith & Life Resources, 2005), and *Sing the Story* (Faith & Life Resources, 2007).

The content for this book was sponsored jointly by Mennonite Women USA and Mennonite Women Canada.

To order or request information, please call 1-800-245-7894
or visit www.MennoMedia.org.

19 18 17 16 15   10 9 8 7 6 5 4 3 2 1

 MennoMedia

Contents

Preface   5

A Guide to Spark: Igniting Your God-Given Creativity   7

1. Genesis 1:1–2:3   11

2. Genesis 1:26-28; 2:4-25   15

3. Exodus 35:30–36:7   19

4. Psalm 117   23

5. Luke 15:1-10   27

6. Matthew 25:14-30   31

7. Matthew 6:25-34   35

8. Romans 12   39

9. I Corinthians 12:1-11   43

10. I Corinthians 10:31; 15:58; Ephesians 6:7; Colossians 3:17 . .   47

11. Philippians 4:4-9   51

12. 2 Timothy 1:1-14   55

13. Closing Worship: Creativity Continues
Psalm 148   59

Resources   65

About Mennonite Women Canada   67

About Mennonite Women USA   69

About the Writer   71

Preface

I've long been fascinated with creating and the creative process, certainly long before I had the language to describe what those things meant. In infancy and early childhood, as we play with sounds and discover the world around us, all of us live like artists, discovering and experimenting with words, colors, shapes, and different forms of self-expression. That creativity continued to grow in me as I wrote my first poems in elementary school, experimented with different recipes as a young bride, studied theology and deepened my appreciation of God as our great Creator, wrote in my personal journal and for publication.

Two years ago, when I joined Pinterest (a popular online bulletin board tool), "Creativity" became one of my first boards, serving as a place to explore creativity in a more deliberate way, to curate various online resources on creativity, and to savor great quotes. So when I received the invitation to write a Bible study series for Mennonite Women USA and Mennonite Women Canada, I was delighted to see creativity on their list of suggested topics. It seemed to claim me as much as I wanted to claim it.

I've enjoyed developing these studies, and dedicate *Spark* to all creatives and would-be creatives, to all of us made in the image of God and created to create. Thank you to Mennonite Women

Canada and Mennonite Women USA for your invitation and support. Thank you to the wonderful readers of my blog for your observations, comments, and questions. Thank you to my family, friends, and church, who have shaped me more than you know.

When it comes to creativity, I'm acutely aware of the gap between vision and reality, between what we imagine and what we are able to realize. So may God's grace and mercy fill up what is missing in this work and in all our creative endeavors.

April Yamasaki

A *Guide to* Spark: Igniting Your God-Given Creativity

A frame around a painting helps to define it and sets the piece of art apart from the world around it. So too I think of this booklet with its sessions as a frame—defining a space of time for creative reflection that's set apart from our regular daily activities. As a frame, *Spark* is made up of 12 study sessions, a worship celebration, this guide section, and a list of further resources.

Within that frame, there's plenty of room for your own creativity—on your own or with a group, for a weekly study or less frequently, to focus on the sessions or parts most appropriate for your context, to freely adapt and add your own ideas. Spark provides the frame, but you decide on the more specific content. So feel free to explore, experiment, and enjoy *Spark: Igniting Your God-Given Creativity*.

IN EACH SESSION:

Overview: an introduction to the session;

Visual: a visual and worship focus, often incorporating supplies to be used as part of *Integrating* or *Sending*;

Gathering: designed to focus attention with a story, Scripture, litany, or in other ways;

Deepening: a reflection centered on Scripture;

Integrating: questions for pondering and discussion, plus a creative exercise to do in a group setting and/or later at home;

Sending: one or two suggested songs, prayers, or other sending activity.

SOME WAYS TO ADAPT THIS MATERIAL:

- Add journaling and silence to any session after the *Gathering* and before moving on to *Deepening* with the following journal prompts: What do I bring to this time? What do I hope for?

- Turn any session into an inductive Bible study by following these three basic steps:

  Observe—What do you observe in this text? *Who* is doing *what*, *where*, *when*, and *why*?

  Interpret—What is the significance of these observations for understanding this text?

  Apply—How does this apply to our lives today?

- Allow time to engage the ideas presented in *Deepening*: What do you affirm? What would you express differently? How does it resonate with or differ from your own understanding and experience?

- Personalize the time for creative expression by thinking about your unique creative interests and those of your group. Invite those with particular interest or skill to present and lead a creative exercise. If you make stained glass or build birdhouses, or whatever you do, use this opportunity to share your gift.

- For any of the suggested songs, feel free to read the words instead; substitute or add other songs familiar to your group; find recordings of choral or instrumental music for listening and reflection.

- See the list of resources (p. 65-66) for full reference information for all quotes and resources cited. Consult these for additional quotes and ideas to add to your sessions.

one · · · · · · · · · · · · · · · ·

Genesis 1:1–2:3

God is the original Artist

OVERVIEW

In 2013 when the Pennsylvania State University partnered with Coursera to offer an online course on creativity, innovation, and change, over 130,000 students from over 190 countries signed up. When former megachurch pastor and now bestselling author Rob Bell taped his first television talk show for the Oprah Winfrey Network, he chose creativity as his opening theme.

Creativity shows itself in all of life, from flower arranging, painting, dancing, music, and other classic arts to the development of new technologies. From the microwave oven invented in the 1940s to the latest tablet or smartphone, human creativity continues to flourish with new forms, tools, and techniques. Creativity means creative expression in all areas of life and in the art of living.

Creativity is not a passing fad, and it's not reserved only for a chosen few. As we'll see in these sessions, creativity is fundamental to who God is, and to who we are as human beings made in God's image.

VISUAL

Water fountain, rocks, potted plants, and/or items for a creation collage (see *Integrating #3*)

GATHERING

Genesis 1:1–2:3 tells the story of creation as a series of days, and a second creation story immediately follows in Genesis 2 that we'll explore in our next session. While these are two key texts, Scripture includes other creation accounts as well. In the book of Job, God retells creation from "the foundation of the earth" (Job 38:4) to the "torrents of rain" (Job 38:25) to the eagle that "makes its home in the fastness of the rocky crag" (Job 39:28). John 1:1 echoes the language of Genesis 1:1—"In the beginning"—and the gospel goes on to describe the creation of "all things" (v. 3).

Colossians 1:15-20 describes creation through Jesus Christ, "the firstborn of all creation" (v. 15), through whom all things were created. Revelation 4:11 offers a song of praise to God as Creator: "You are worthy, our Lord and God, to receive glory and honor and power, for you created all things, and by your will they existed and were created." From Genesis to Revelation, God is the great Creator and source of all things.

DEEPENING

Genesis 1 has been explored in various ways. In this series, we look at what this beautifully rich text can teach us about creativity.

This opening chapter of the Bible is a profound confession of God, the great Creator, as the original Artist, creating light and dark, creating life itself. God is the source of all that exists—the clay we mold into pots; the food we cook; the colors we paint; the fabrics, wood, pencils, and other creative materials we use; our eyes that appreciate a beautiful scene; our voices that rise in song; our sense of balance, proportion, and artistry. All our creativity was first created by God.

One of the myths about creativity is that it's only about radically new ideas. But according to British psychologist Michael Kirton, creativity is both "innovative" and "adaptive," both "out of the box" and working within it. When Spencer Silver first created a glue that allowed paper to be attached and then easily peeled off, it was so innovative that no one could see a use for it. But when Art Fry needed something to mark the page of his hymnal for choir practice, he thought of using the glue for a temporary bookmark—it was an example of adaptive creativity, and with it, the Post-it Note was born, the child of both innovative and adaptive creativity.

Creativity might mean coming up with an entirely new kind of glue, *and* it also means adapting it for a specific context. Creativity might mean developing your own exercise routine, *or* it might mean taking a different route to your regular gym class. Creativity might mean coming up with an entirely new recipe, *and* creativity means adapting an existing recipe to make it your own.

In Genesis God creates both ways! Innovation occurred as God created something entirely new: where there was chaos, God created a new order; where there was nothing, God created an entire universe. At the same time, God's creativity was adaptive: the earth brought forth plants, and the plants brought forth fruit and seed; the living creatures reproduced and multiplied.

INTEGRATING

1 . God is the Creator of everything, so all human creativity is really "adaptive." But within that, there seem to be varying degrees of innovation and adaptive creativity. Consider your own experience. Do you tend toward innovation—that is, coming up with new ideas not necessarily related to anyone or anything else, or toward adaptive creativity—that is, adapting ideas to a particular context? Give thanks for both expressions of creativity.

2 . Note the pauses throughout Genesis 1—for evening rest, reflection, and appreciation ("God saw that it was good"), for a seventh day of rest at the end of the week. When I get stuck on a piece of writing, I find it helpful to take a break and do something else while my ideas continue to percolate. Some of my best ideas come while I'm washing dishes or out for a walk. Where and when do you get your ideas? Whether you're working on an art project or in need of creative parenting ideas, problem solving at work or planning a party, how is pausing and resting part of your creative process?

3 . Use photos, magazine pictures, ribbon, buttons, and other items to make a creation collage. You might choose to focus your collage on food, or beautiful colors, or gardening, or other creative expression. Post it on your refrigerator or somewhere else as a daily reminder of God's creativity.

SENDING

- Sing "All Things Bright and Beautiful" (*Hymnal: A Worship Book* #156) or listen to "Creation Calls" by Brian Doerksen.

- Read Psalm 29 responsively, alternating verses, with everyone together on the last verse.

two . . . .

Genesis 1:26-28; 2:4-25

Created in the image of God means
being created to create

OVERVIEW

In Genesis 1, God speaks all of creation into being, and in Genesis 2, God forms human beings by hand. This second creation story paints an intimate and tender picture of God patiently gathering dust and breathing life, taking a rib and fashioning a man and a woman in personal relationship with each other and with God. In contrast to the broad sweep of creation from chaos to created order in Genesis 1, this second account focuses attention on the creation of humankind.

As Father, Son, and Spirit express divine community, so a man and a woman and all of their offspring form a human community. As God is the original Creator and Artist, human beings made in God's image receive a divine spark of creativity. God's blessing commissions them to "be fruitful and multiply, and fill the earth and subdue it; and have dominion" (Genesis 1:28), to explore God's good creation, to be creative and productive, to care for the earth like a garden (Genesis 2:15).

VISUAL

Soil, seeds, gardening gloves, small hand tools, and supplies to create a dish garden (see *Integrating* #3)

GATHERING

Read Psalm 8 as an opening for this session. Notice how the middle verses of this psalm echo Genesis 1 and describe how God has given humankind "dominion" over creation (Genesis 1:26; cf. Psalm 8:3-8): "You have given them dominion over the works of your hands" (Psalm 8:6). Too often, however, the emphasis has fallen on human dominion as doing whatever we please to the point of domination—and even destruction—of the natural world.

In contrast, Psalm 8 reminds us that we too are the work of God's hands: "*You* have made them. . . . *You* have given them" (vv. 5-6, emphasis added). Whatever dominion we have been given belongs first to God, and has in turn been entrusted to us. What's more, the psalm begins with praise to God: "O LORD, our Sovereign, how majestic is your name in all the earth!" (v. 1) and ends in the same way: "O LORD, our Sovereign, how majestic is your name in all the earth!" (v. 9). The repetition at the beginning and end of the psalm reminds us that human agency and creativity begin and end with God and take shape under God's sovereignty.

DEEPENING

While Genesis 1 and 2 focus on different aspects of creation, both offer vivid illustrations of creativity, first in God's work of creation and then in human creativity. In Genesis 1, God creates light and calls it Day, separates the light from darkness, and calls the darkness Night (1:5). As creation continues to unfold, God also names Sky (1:8) and Earth (1:10). In Genesis 2, the first act of human creativity is to name the animals (2:20).

Genesis 1 unfolds like a hymn of praise with a constant refrain of delight: "God saw that it was good" (1:10, 12, 18, 21, 25, 31). Genesis 2 ends in delight when the man finally receives and recognizes the woman as his partner: "This at last is bone of my bones and flesh of my flesh" (2:23). The man welcomes the woman as a fellow creature and partner in God's good garden.

In Genesis 1, God gives humanity dominion over creation, and in Genesis 2 this dominion is expressed in vulnerability with each other and with God, a dominion exercised with love and care as God lovingly and carefully created humankind. Human creativity means the man and the woman sharing their lives together and tending the earth like a garden: imagining, dreaming, discussing, planning, record keeping, working with tools and inventing new ones, planting seeds, weeding, watering, harvesting, eating the fruits of their labor, celebrating, sharing with others, practicing hospitality, and expressing themselves in many other creative ways.

INTEGRATING

1. Creativity is about art, and yet it is also so much more than any art form. Creativity is a way of life that we might call artful living. As Hans Rookmaaker writes in *The Creative Gift*: "Creativity means growing bulbs, designing a new car, building a computer, discovering certain relationships within molecules, or writing a sermon. All these activities and a thousand more, like town planning, architecture, road construction, but also office work and cooking" (p. 74).

There are countless ways to express our creativity every day. Share one way that you have expressed your creativity in this past week. Share one way that you can be intentionally creative in the coming week.

2 . In both Genesis 1 and 2, creative work brings great delight, celebration, and good rest at the end of the day. But it does not come without good effort. Think of something that you have created. Surely it took time and patience. It takes more time and effort to cook a meal from scratch than to zap a frozen dinner in the microwave. It takes time to craft and recraft the cadence of a poem or to use watercolors on a canvas. How do you find time to be creative?

Are there some things that you need to stop doing to allow more creative space in your life?

3 . Create a simple dish garden in a shallow bowl, with pebbles on the bottom for good drainage, then a layer of soil with bulbs or small plants, decorative rocks, or other items. Water your garden and reflect on the care it will require to grow and flourish. What difference does it make to understand dominion as the responsibility to care for a garden versus the license to do as we please?

SENDING

- Sing "Morning Has Broken" (*Hymnal: A Worship Book* #648) or "Creation Is a Song" (*Sing the Journey* #24).

- Create your own litany by inviting each person to complete this sentence: "O Lord, I praise you for _____." Then respond each time as a group with the refrain from Psalm 8: "O LORD, our Sovereign, how majestic is your name in all the earth!"

- Give thanks for the creative experiences of this past week, and ask for God's leading as you seek to be intentionally creative in the coming week.

three. . . . .

Exodus 35:30–36:7

> "You can't use up creativity;
> the more you use, the more you have."
> —MAYA ANGELOU

OVERVIEW

In my congregation, the finance committee reports to our church council throughout the year, and then in November the whole congregation receives a reminder about year-end giving. But what if our finance committee would say instead, "Please don't give any more. We have more than enough to meet the church budget, for all of our wider church commitments, and to start any new ministry. Stop giving because we just can't handle any more."

That's what happened when the Hebrew people built their tabernacle in the wilderness. They brought so many materials and had so many volunteers to do the work that Moses had to tell them to stop: "No man or woman is to make anything else as an offering for the sanctuary" (Exodus 36:6).

When it comes to creativity, God gives more than enough—God gives an abundance, and keeps on giving. As Maya Angelou puts it, "You can't use up creativity; the more you use, the more you have."

VISUAL

Beautifully colored fabrics of different textures and designs

GATHERING

The Scripture reading for this session sums up Exodus 35 and 36. As the people prepared to make the tabernacle and furnish it with an altar, vestments for the priests, vessels for incense, and other sacred objects, Exodus 35:22-28 lists their many different offerings. Instead of donations by cash, check, or debit or credit card as we might make today, the people brought their donations in kind: acacia wood to build the sanctuary and the altar; gold jewelry that could be melted down and made into lampstands; precious stones, silver, bronze; yarn and goat hair that could be spun and sewn into curtains; spices for incense; olive oil for burning.

The people also brought their abilities. Exodus 35:29–36:2 names Bezalel and Oholiab, but they were just two of the many skilled craftspeople, designers, embroiderers, weavers, metalworkers, woodworkers, and other artisans. The offerings kept coming, and the people kept coming. Instead of having to do more with less, God's abundance meant that they could do more with more, to be creative more and more.

What was their secret? How might we experience creativity that never runs out?

DEEPENING

The Hebrew people lived and travelled as a nomad people out in the wilderness. How could they possibly make a tabernacle and furnish it? I can almost hear their complaining, "We're wandering in the wilderness. We have limited resources. We don't know what to do. Why don't we wait until we reach the Promised Land?" But instead of focusing on themselves and on all that they did not have, they focused their attention on God and God's provision. "This is the thing that the LORD has commanded," Moses said to them (Exodus 35:4, emphasis added).

At the same time, the people were "willing," which literally means to be lifted up or to be stirred up (Exodus 35:5, 21, 22, 26, 29, 36:2). When I bake bread, I stir together flour, honey, oil, water, a bit of salt, a bit of yeast, then knead it, let it rest in a warm place, and the bread dough rises. Like a baker kneading bread, God stirred up the dough—God stirred up the people, and they rose with a willing yes and yes and yes until there was more than enough.

Together, the people did what they could, each one bringing an offering. Whoever had gold jewelry brought gold jewelry. Whoever had olive oil brought olive oil. Whoever could work with wood offered their woodworking skills. Whoever could weave gave their time to weaving.

Of course, creative living takes time and effort, whether you're making a tabernacle or an evening meal, playing Lego with your children or making a scrapbook, building a house or writing a poem. And it's easy to come up with excuses:

- I don't have time.
- I don't feel like it.
- I need to clean up the kitchen first.
- So-and-so can do it better.
- So-and-so is more creative.

If living a creative life is all up to me, there are a thousand reasons why it can't be done. But like the Hebrew people, for creativity that never runs out, I need to shift my focus from myself and my own resources to God's provision. Instead of offering excuses, I can offer what I have. Instead of denying or belittling God's gift, I can be willing for God to stir my heart and use me.

INTEGRATING

1 . In what areas of life is God stirring you to live more creatively? Write down the excuses preventing you from moving more strongly in that direction. Then deliberately shift your attention from your excuses to God's provision by shredding and recycling your list. Make a new list of all the creative materials and skills that God has given you. Keep this new list in your Bible as a reminder of God's gifting, and plan to practice one of the skills.

2 . The artist painting alone on the seashore might be one expression of creativity, but in our Exodus text, the Hebrew people create the tabernacle and its furnishings together. How is community part of your creative process? In what ways can you offer your creative gifts to your community?

3 . Bake bread or muffins this week. Breathe in the rich aroma, and breathe out a prayer of thanks for God's provision. Give your baked goods away as a creative offering and reminder of God's abundance.

SENDING

- Sing "God, Whose Giving Knows No Ending" (*Hymnal: A Worship Book* #383).

- Pray in unison:
  God, you are stirring within us.
  Make us bold to create,
  and bold to offer our gifts in community.
  We confess that we have not always accepted
  the creative ones among us.
  We have not always recognized
  your gifts in others and even in ourselves.
  Forgive us our failures,
  and open our eyes and hearts
  to your stirring among us. Amen.

four . . . .

Psalm 117

Scripture is a God-breathed work of creativity

OVERVIEW

Not long ago I received a note that said, "The trouble with the church is too much poetry and not enough Bible." I understand the concern for biblical literacy, and I long for more of the Bible in churches and in everyday life, too. But poetry and the Bible are not mutually exclusive. In fact, the Bible is full of poetry. The Psalms, the book of Job, and much of the Prophets take the form of Hebrew poetry. What's more, in addition to poetry, there are many other creative expressions in Scripture—stories, songs, dreams, letters, the building of the tabernacle and the temple, and much more!

VISUAL

Copies of the Bible in traditional book formats, electronic versions, children's Bibles, such as *Shine On: A Story Bible*.

GATHERING

In his preface to the *German Psalter* (1531), Martin Luther said that the Psalms "might well be entitled a Little Bible, wherein everything contained in the entire Bible is beautifully and briefly comprehended." The Psalms speak of God's mercy and goodness: "O give thanks to the LORD, for he is good; for his steadfast love endures forever" (Psalm 107:1). They acknowledge God as the source of salvation. "Restore to me the joy of your salvation, and sustain in me a willing spirit" (Psalm 51:12). They embrace all of life, from praise to lament, in times of worship and in times of desperation, from calm reflection to bitter complaint and anger.

My all-time favorite is Psalm 23. It's the first psalm I ever memorized. I've read it many times in different versions for my own reflection and prayer. I've read it in homes as a blessing and in hospitals for comfort, at church for worship and at gravesides for a final farewell. I thought I might get tired of it by now, but the beauty and power of the language still move me after all these years, and I'm still learning what it means to trust in the Lord as my shepherd.

What is your favorite psalm, and why? What has it taught you? What are you still learning?

DEEPENING

In the Bible, there are many psalms of praise with a similar poetic form:
- beginning with an opening call to praise, which serves as an introduction;
- then the body of the psalm outlining the reasons for praising God;
- followed by a concluding call to praise, which often repeats the introduction.

For example, Psalm 113 begins and ends with the words "Praise the LORD!" (vv. 1, 9), and in between it describes God's "glory above the heavens" (v. 4) and praises God who "raises the poor

... and lifts the needy" (v. 7). Psalm 103 begins and ends with the words "Bless the LORD, O my soul" (vv. 1, 22), and in between offers some of the reasons why: God's mercy, forgiveness, and blessing (vv. 2-22).

In some of these psalms, the reasons for praising God can go on for 10, 20, or more verses. For example, Psalm 106 begins and ends with "Praise the LORD" (vv. 1, 48), and in between there are 46 other verses recounting God's wonderful work. In contrast, Psalm 117 is the shortest praise psalm, with just two verses. It follows the same pattern, but in a much shorter form: beginning and ending with "Praise the LORD" (vv. 1, 2), with just one verse in between. Why do we praise the Lord? "For great is his love toward us, and the faithfulness of the LORD endures forever" (v. 2).

The poetry of praise may be longer or shorter, but always remains grounded in who God is and what God has done. The Hebrew word *hallel* means literally "to be boastful" or "to be excited in joy." We might think of it as a cheer, like when our team wins the big game in overtime. *Hallelu* is plural, as if you're in a room full of friends, shouting for joy and including them all, congratulating them and your whole team on TV, even though they can't hear you. And *jah* is a shortened form for "the Lord," and completes the thought. *Hallelujah*—let's all praise the Lord! For the ancient Hebrew, the poetry of praise is always directed toward God.

INTEGRATING

1. The psalms of praise are among the most beautiful passages in Scripture. But the Psalms also include more difficult and disturbing imagery, like Psalm 137:9 and Psalm 139:19-22. Must all art be beautiful? Why or why not? What role does beauty play in art and creative living?

2. As a God-breathed work, the Bible has inspired sculpture, painting, calligraphy, architecture, choir cantatas, rock operas, dance, hymns and spiritual songs, instrumentals, novels, plays, poems, films, and other works of art. Yet the church has sometimes been ambivalent or even opposed to art and artists. Is there a hierarchy of the arts in the church today, with some forms of art more accepted and others less so? Do we need to be more cautious about some forms of art than others?

3. Write your own poetry of praise following the basic structure of the Hebrew praise psalm. Begin and end with a line of praise or a simple "hallelujah," then insert one or more lines giving reasons. For an added challenge, you may wish to experiment with another characteristic form of Hebrew poetry, which includes pairs of lines that echo one another. So in Psalm 117:1, the first line is "Praise the LORD, all you nations!" and the second line repeats the thought in slightly different words: "Extol him, all you peoples!"

SENDING

- Even if your poetry of praise remains unfinished, share at least a line or two with your group as a shared offering of praise to God.

- Sing "God of the Bible" (*Sing the Journey* #27).

- Conclude with this psalm of praise:
    Praise God, the great Creator!
    For life and health,
    strength of body and spirit,
    for the gift of creativity,
    and God-given imagination.
    Praise God!

five . . . .

Luke 15:1-10

"Jesus was an artist."
—DONALD C. MANN

OVERVIEW

Jesus proclaimed the good news of God's kingdom in creative ways: telling stories, answering questions with wit and humor, forming a community of disciples. He imagined the kingdom of God like a mustard seed (Luke 13:18-19) and yeast (Luke 13:20-21). He described himself as a farmer scattering seed and his hearers as different types of soil (Matthew 13:1-23). When a lawyer asked him "Teacher, which commandment in the law is the greatest?" he sidestepped the trap and responded with a two-part commandment to love God and neighbor, and so summarized the entire law (Matthew 22:34-40).

Jesus' creative and compelling call to God's kingdom appealed to fishermen, tax collectors, prostitutes, household servants, widows, poor people and women of means, people struggling with mental and physical illness, a military man, a Samaritan woman, and many more. Who but a Master Artist could envision their potential? Who but a Master Artist could take an apparently random group of disciples and transform them into passionate and compassionate witnesses?

VISUAL

Streamers, party favors, other signs of celebration (see *Integrating* #2)

GATHERING

In Luke's gospel, Jesus' parables and healings often appear in pairs. In Luke 4, Jesus heals a man with an unclean spirit (4:33-35), and then heals Simon's mother-in-law (4:38-39). In Luke 7, he heals the slave of a centurion (7:1-10), then reaches out to a widow to raise her son from the dead (7:11-15). In Luke 18, Jesus tells two parables on prayer: one about a persistent widow (18:1-8) and the other about a tax collector who humbled himself before God (18:9-14). Here in Luke 15 we have another pair of parables, this time centered on searching for a lost sheep (15:3-7) and a lost coin (15:8-10).

Now it might seem repetitious—even unnecessary—for the gospel to include these pairs of stories. Why make the same point twice? Why not just say it once and then move on? But the pattern in the gospel suggests that this pairing is deliberate. Jesus as healer restores both men and women to health and wholeness and calls both women and men to persistent prayer. In the two stories of the lost sheep and the lost coin, the God Who Never Gives Up keeps searching for all those who are missing.

DEEPENING

In Jesus' first story, the shepherd owns a hundred sheep. When one goes missing, he leaves the ninety-nine to go searching for the one lost sheep. In the second story, the woman has ten coins, with each coin worth about 10 days' wages. When one coin goes missing, she searches for it through her entire house.

This man and woman are not religious leaders. While they have enough to live on, they are not especially wealthy. They're people who work for themselves, who don't have servants to run after a lost sheep or to sweep the floors for a lost coin. They search personally and diligently until they find what was lost. They're so excited by their great finds that they call their friends and neighbors to celebrate with them. They wouldn't normally be counted among the superheroes of the Bible, but they illustrate how God searches for us.

The two short parables go together, linked quite simply by the word *or*. There is no introduction to the second story, no preamble to separate the two. In both, Jesus draws a word picture that invites us to use our imagination. Suppose this would happen or suppose this other thing would happen, says Jesus. How might we respond?

Imagine yourself into one of these two stories. Are you the sheep lost in the wilderness, or the lost coin caught between two stones? Are you the shepherd, or the woman desperately searching for something or someone? Are you a bystander, listening to the story but not really part of the action? Or one of the friends and neighbors called alongside to celebrate? What other role might you imagine for yourself?

Then reimagine a time when you lost something. What were your thoughts and feelings? Did you search for your missing item as diligently as the man looked for his sheep and the woman looked for her lost coin? Why or why not? What does their search tell you about God's intentions toward us?

INTEGRATING

1 . Immediately after these stories of the lost sheep and the lost coin, Jesus tells a third story about a lost son. Read Luke 15:11-32. How do the three stories together enrich one another? What do they teach about God?

2 . Imagine you are hosting a party for the man who found his lost sheep or the woman who found her lost coin. How would you decorate? What food would you serve? Would you play games or have other entertainment? Be creative, and plan to celebrate!

3 . A parable uses familiar objects or people to tease us into a lesson about God's kingdom. Write your own parable by starting with 10 minutes of freewriting about an everyday object that has some spiritual significance to you. As you begin, feel free to set aside any concern about good grammar or spelling. You can always take time for revising later; for now just get your thoughts on paper. What object will you choose? What spiritual story does it tell?

SENDING

- Sing "Amazing Grace" (*Hymnal: A Worship Book* #143) or "Gentle Shepherd, Come and Lead Us" (*Hymnal: A Worship Book* #352).

- Share your parables with one another; if yours isn't ready, tell the group what object you have chosen, and why.

- Pray for those who are missing: for the children and adults reported missing in your own community and country, and for those displaced and missing around the world due to disaster and war.

Matthew 25:14-30

Creativity is best measured in faithfulness
and joy

OVERVIEW

Once again, Jesus uses wit and creativity to tell a story that makes a point. On one level, the story is about making money, but Jesus tells it as a story about God's kingdom. A man goes on a journey, leaving his servants in charge of his property, and once he returns, he calls them to account for their actions

What Jesus says also applies to the gift of creativity—it's not the same as the sums of money left with the master's servants, but creativity is entrusted to us by God, and we are also responsible to use it wisely and well. What then might we learn from the two servants who multiplied what they had been given, and from the fearful servant who lost everything?

VISUAL

A large pitcher of water, an empty medium-sized pitcher (set on a dish to catch any overflow), assorted glasses (one for each participant) containing small amounts of water

GATHERING

Imagine Jesus' parable retold in contemporary terms: A multibillionaire and investment guru decided to go away on a trip. So he entrusted some of his investments to three employees: $5 million to the first, $2 million to the second, and $1 million to the third.

The two employees with the $5 million and $2 million immediately invested their money, and doubled it. But the employee with the $1 million hid it in the back corner of his office.

When the investment guru returned, the first employee said, "Good news—your $5 million is now worth $10 million." The guru said, "Excellent! I will give you even more responsibility. Come and celebrate with me!" The second employee said, "Good news—your $2 million is now worth $4 million." The guru said, "Excellent! I will give you even more responsibility. Come and celebrate with me!" The third employee said, "I know your reputation as one of the most successful investors in the world, so I was afraid and hid your million dollars, and now here it is." The guru said, "You're fired! I will give that million dollars to someone else. Clear out your desk immediately!"

DEEPENING

Just as the master in Jesus' parable entrusted his servants with his property, God has entrusted us with the gift of creativity.

Creativity is a trust. It doesn't belong to us. Like the servants in Jesus' parable, like a good investment broker today, we don't act only for ourselves. Our creative talents and skills are only ours in trust, to be exercised in God's service and for the good of others.

Creativity is meant to be used. According to rabbinic law, if a person buried money in a secret location, that person was freed of any responsibility. So when the servant buried his master's money, he seemed to be saying, "I'm no longer responsible." But the master expected him to use the money at least to earn some interest. We too are responsible to put our creativity to good use.

Creativity means taking risks. I can just imagine the fearful servant muttering to himself, "What if I invest this money, and get little or no return? What if I end up losing it all? I can't take that risk. Better just to bury it." Our creativity can also get buried under excuses and fear. I'm too old. I'm too young. What if I make a mistake? What if I fail? What if I'm misunderstood, or even rejected by others? In the face of these and other fears, Jesus invites us to risk time, effort, and creative energy.

Creativity takes enthusiasm and initiative. Verse 16 provides this detail, "The one who had received the five talents went off *at once* and traded with them" (emphasis added). This servant didn't hesitate. He didn't waste time congratulating himself on receiving a larger share than the others, or wondering why he hadn't been given even more. He focused his considerable energy and got right to work.

Creativity leads to joy. The first servant made over twice as much money for his master as the second servant. But in spiritual terms, both were equally faithful, and both were rewarded with joy. So too our creative efforts are not about how much money we make, how many rave reviews we receive, or who is more successful. Creativity is best measured in faithfulness and joy.

INTEGRATING

1 . The fearful servant seemed to be paralyzed by his fear, unable even to invest his master's money. We're not told what the other two servants thought of their master, or whether they too were afraid, but they were at least able to respond in responsible and creative ways. Does fear fuel your creativity, or does it tend to paralyze you?

2 . One musician says that she feels able to take more risks when she plays with musicians whom she trusts. A friend feels freer to experiment with recipes when she's cooking for her own family than when she has guests. How is trust part of your creative process—trusting God, trusting the process, trusting yourself and others?

3 . I don't know who started "Writer Wednesday," but designating the day encourages me to write. I've sometimes thought about renaming the other days of the week, too. Magnificent Make-It-Yourself Monday could lend itself to all kinds of creative projects. Fifteen-Minute Friday could be a day to take 15 minutes to start something new. As a creative exercise, give each day of the week your own unique designation.

SENDING

- Pray together:
  For the measure of grace and gifts you have given us,
  O God, we give you thanks.
  > (*Each woman takes a glass of water and pours it into the empty pitcher.*)
  Multiply these treasures with enthusiasm and joy,
  > (*Leader pours water from the large pitcher to fill the medium pitcher so that it overflows.*)
  O God, we give you thanks.

- Pray "We Clutch Our Tiny Bits of Faith" (*Sing the Journey* #152).

- Sing "You Shall Go Out with Joy" (*Hymnal: A Worship Book* #427).

seven . . . .

Matthew 6:25-34

Worry is a misuse of creativity

OVERVIEW

When I first started dreaming about this series on creativity, I invited readers of my blog to submit their comments, questions, and suggested resources. Several recommended books that were new to me, including *Art and Fear: Observations on the Perils (and Rewards) of Artmaking*, by David Bayles and Ted Orland. The suggestion came with this strong endorsement from a reader: "I return to it when I'm stuck, and when I need to think about what it means to create."

The authors say that their book is about "ordinary art"—not the art of the prodigy or the genius or the professional, but the kind of art that any of us might make—and they explore the fears that sometimes stop us from making anything at all. These include fears that we might be less than perfect, that we're pretending, that we're untalented, fears that others might not understand, accept, or approve of what we're doing.

Even if all those things are true, why should we worry? Worrying won't make us more talented or make anyone else understand us better. We might even say that worry is a misuse of our creativity as we imagine all the things that could go wrong.

VISUAL

A large, empty bowl surrounded by smooth stones

GATHERING

Worry seems to make everything worse. If you have high blood pressure, worry can make it even higher. If you can't sleep, worry can shorten or interrupt your sleep even more. If you have family troubles, money problems, a delicate situation at your job or church, a flood in your basement, a computer that won't cooperate, or whatever other challenges you face—worry can make them harder to deal with, and harder for others to deal with you. Worry is so common that it's been called the disease of the 21st century for the Western world. We even worry about worrying too much!

Matthew 6:25-34 tells us that such worrying is not unique to us. The content of our worrying might vary—from general health concerns to that very specific biopsy that no one knows about but you and your doctor; from how to resolve that problem at work to where to hold the family reunion. Worry seems to be everywhere, anytime. It can make us hesitate, procrastinate, or give up altogether.

DEEPENING

Jesus uses some creative illustrations from the natural world to address a number of basic human fears:

- Will I have enough to eat and drink (v. 25)?
- Will I have enough clothes (v. 25) and the right kind (vv. 29-30)?
- How long will I live (v. 27)?
- What will tomorrow bring (v. 34)?

As I imagine Jesus walking through the fields with his disciples, and sitting on the mountainside to teach, I can appreciate the way he addresses these concerns by referring to the birds and the lilies. Just as God cares for them, God also cares for us. Yet in the 21st century, some birds have been hunted to extinction or become weighed down and unable to fly because of oil tanker spills. Plant life suffers from pollution and climate change. As humans we have caused much damage. The world has changed since the time of Jesus. Yet the point he makes still holds true: God knows our needs and cares for us. For Jesus the antidote to worry is trust in God and seeking God's kingdom.

But what does it mean to seek God's kingdom? I sometimes wish that Jesus had been more specific, but he never set out any kind of five-year plan, never gave the 10 surefire steps to make God's kingdom happen. Instead, Jesus used everyday illustrations and stories to stimulate imagination, provoke questions, inspire trust in God's Spirit, and engage his hearers in wondering, praying, working, experimenting, and living. All that and more is what it means to seek God's kingdom, and when we are fully engaged in those ways, there is no room for worry. Worrying cannot give us a longer life or a better life. It can't make us more ready to face tomorrow, whatever tomorrow may bring.

INTEGRATING

1 . **Worrying takes imagination**. When I'm worried, I may find it more difficult to create anything else but more worry. But when my imagination is fully engaged in a creative project, my worries tend to recede into the background. How are worry, imagination, and creativity related in your experience?

2 . **In my Bible**, Matthew 6:25-34 bears the title "Do Not Worry." Phrased more positively, it could also be "Set Good Priorities."

What priority does Jesus give in these verses? How does setting priorities help to dispel worry?

3 . Make flowers using several colored sheets of tissue paper for the petals and a pipe cleaner for the stem. Find simple instructions on the Internet or in another resource. Place the flowers together in a vase, and set them beside the empty bowl as part of your visual focus.

SENDING

Pass out slips of paper to be used during this guided prayer. Allow time for silence as indicated, to breathe deeply, and rest in God's presence.

- Pray:
  (Invite each woman to write her worries on one or more slips of paper and then place them in the bowl as a sign of releasing her worry to God. Each then takes a smooth stone as a symbol of trust in God. Take as much time as the group needs for this, with shorter periods of silence to follow. Be sure to destroy the slips of paper after the session.)
  Cast all your anxiety on God who cares for you.
  (silence)
  O God, the giver of every good gift, transform our worry into trust.
  (silence)
  Transform our worry into seeking God's kingdom.
  (silence)
  Transform our worry into living one day at a time.
  (silence)
  Amen.
- Sing "Seek Ye First the Kingdom of God" (*Hymnal: A Worship Book* #324) or "10,000 Reasons (Bless the Lord)" by Matt Redman.

eight . . . .

Romans 12

> ## "There is nothing more truly artistic than to love people."
> —VINCENT VAN GOGH

OVERVIEW

Romans 12 lists some of the creative gifts that God has given us, along with some "best practices" for how we might put them to good use. Verses 6-8 mention the gifts of prophecy, service, teaching, encouragement, generosity, leadership, compassion. Other gifts appear in 1 Corinthians 12, Ephesians 4, and there are many more: music, listening, helping, cooking, building—a wonderfully endless list of being and doing given to us by God and meant to be used in wonderfully creative ways.

Romans 12 identifies seven of the best ways to use our gifts:
1. give your gift first to God (v. 1);
2. allow God to transform it (v. 2);
3. use it with discernment (vv. 2-3);
4. use your gift alongside the gifts of others (vv. 4-8);
5. do good (vv. 9, 13-21);
6. love (v. 9-11);
7. pray (v. 12).

This session focuses more on love, on creativity as an expression of love, which the apostle Paul describes as "a still more excellent way" (1 Corinthians 12:31).

VISUAL

Photos of people from your church directory or framed family photos brought by women in the group

GATHERING

My husband and I chose a print of Vincent Van Gogh's *The Starry Night* to hang above the mantel of our fireplace. In the foreground of the painting, a large cedar tree dominates the landscape and points to heaven. Moon and stars seem to pulse and swirl above the hillsides and sleeping village. Someday I'd love to see the original, which hangs in the Museum of Modern Art in New York City.

Today, *The Starry Night* and Van Gogh's other paintings are among the most well-known and most expensive paintings in the world. But during his lifetime, the artist was unknown and struggling— with debt, with his mental and emotional health, with his art. In one letter, he thanks his brother, Theo, for sending him a 50-franc note and asks him to send more money. "You are kind to painters," he writes, "and I tell you, the more I think it over, the more I feel that there is nothing more truly artistic than to love people."

DEEPENING

The first 11 chapters of Romans focus on God's good news in Jesus Christ, and the last 5 chapters focus on living out that good news. In other words, the first 11 chapters describe the "what" of the gospel, and the last 5 chapters outline the "so what" of Christian living. The hinge between these two parts of the book is "I appeal to you therefore," in Romans 12:1. Because of everything in the first part of the book, "therefore" everything else follows.

That means when Romans 12:10 says, "love one another," we need to understand that love in light of the first part of the letter: "God's love has been poured into our hearts through the Holy Spirit that has been given to us" (Romans 5:5); "God proves his love for us in that while we still were sinners Christ died for us" (Romans 5:8); nothing "will be able to separate us from the love of God in Christ Jesus our Lord" (Romans 8:39). Loving others does not take place in a vacuum, but as a response to God's love that sustains and enables us to love others.

In Romans 12, love means honoring other people (v. 10), consistently praying for them (v. 12), giving in response to needs (v. 13), sharing hospitality (v. 13), blessing even those who are against you (v. 14), sharing joys and sorrows (v. 15), living in harmony and humility (vv. 16, 18), doing good (vv. 17-21).

One woman describes her painting as a hobby, but I see it quite clearly as a creative ministry of love. She hung one of her paintings at the hair salon where she works so others might enjoy it, and when one senior couple going through a hard time admired it, she gave it to them. She donated four paintings for a cancer fundraiser. She's certainly not as famous as Van Gogh, but in the art of loving people, she is just as much an artist.

A young couple in my church have started an open house Sunday dinner. It began as a Facebook group with this announcement: "We are opening our house EVERY WEEK for whoever feels like joining us. All are welcome, so feel free to bring along friends and family too. Just let us know if you are planning to come, and if you are able please bring something to share. We will generally be making simple food, like soup—so buns, salad, dessert, and drinks are ideas of what you can bring." Such creative community building is another kind of art that expresses genuine love.

INTEGRATING

1. Just before the list of gifts in Romans 12, verse 6 acknowledges that "We have gifts that differ according to the grace given to us." Differences enrich us, but can also give rise to competition and jealousy. How does the love described in this chapter guard against this?

2. Take some time for quiet reflection, and consider the photos on display. Hold each person or group before God in prayer, reflecting on God's love for them, giving thanks for their different gifts, and lifting up any needs.

3. Write messages of encouragement on separate sticky notes; for example, "God loves you!"; "Have a beautiful day"; "I appreciate you." Then find a creative way to share these—in your child's lunch box, on your neighbor's door, in your coworker's cubicle, on lockers at the gym—wherever you would like to express God's love.

SENDING

- Sing "Will You Let Me Be Your Servant?" (*Hymnal: A Worship Book* #307) or "Multiply Your Love" by Andy Park.

- Stand in a circle and join hands while you listen to the love chapter, 1 Corinthians 13.

- Pray God's love especially for those who are sick or lonely, and ask for God's leading in offering yourself and your creativity in loving others.

nine **. . . . .**

1 Corinthians 12:1-11

The Holy Spirit inspires creativity for the common good

OVERVIEW

The last time I preached on this text, I called my sermon "What Is a Spiritual Gift, and Do I Have One?" I made it a pointed question to explore these verses in a personal and practical way. We learned that the word *spiritual* literally means "of the spirit." So a "spiritual gift" is not "of my own personal ability" or "of my education." It might begin with some natural talent. It might be nurtured by education and developed by training and experience. But spiritual gifts are so much more!

In this text, spiritual gifts are given and led by God's Spirit. They express "Jesus is Lord" (vv. 1-3) and work for the common good (vv. 4-11). Spiritual gifts serve God, and by them we serve one another and bear witness to the world. And yes, each of us has been gifted in just that way: "To *each* is given the manifestation of the Spirit for the common good" (v. 7, emphasis added).

VISUAL

Origami doves made in advance as samples, and colorful origami paper (see *Integrating* #3)

GATHERING

First Corinthians 12:1-11 contrasts the "varieties of gifts, but the same Spirit" (v. 4), the "varieties of services, but the same Lord" (v. 5), the "varieties of activities, but it is the same God" (v. 6). After listing a number of different gifts (vv. 8-10), the text concludes, "All these are the work of one and the same Spirit" (v. 11 NIV). So while my Bible calls this section of verses "Spiritual Gifts," they could just as easily be titled "The Same Spirit."

By speaking repeatedly of the many gifts and the one Spirit, the text reminds us of both gifts and giver. By listing particular gifts, it reminds us of both gifted individuals and the way that gifts are meant to work together. So while we might well ask, "What is a spiritual gift? Do *I* have one?" we might also ask, "What gifts have we been given? How are we to use them? How might we work together for the good of all?"

DEEPENING

As a first-year university student, I enrolled in a course that combined English, literature, history, and philosophy. For my first paper, I wrote a Bible-as-literature essay on the book of Exodus, and at one point referred to the Holy Spirit. When I met with my professor to discuss my paper, she said, "You can't say that. The Holy Spirit is a New Testament idea. You're writing about the Old Testament. The Holy Spirit wasn't invented yet."

With all due respect to my professor, the Holy Spirit was not some kind of late invention by New Testament writers. From the very beginning, in Genesis 1, the Spirit of God was present in creation. God's Spirit stirred the people to give and express their creativity in assembling the tabernacle and its furnishings (Exodus 35–36). God's Spirit moved Isaiah, Jeremiah, and others to speak out for peace, justice, and mercy. Psalm 139:8-10 describes how the Holy Spirit is everywhere:

> If I ascend to heaven, you are there;
>> if I make my bed in Sheol, you are there.
> If I take the wings of the morning
>> and settle at the farthest limits of the sea,
> even there your hand shall lead me,
>> and your right hand shall hold me fast.

In the New Testament, the Holy Spirit continues to be present and at work everywhere. In the gospel accounts, it's by the power of God's Spirit that Jesus heals the sick, casts out demons, and proclaims the reign of God (Matthew 12:28; Luke 3:22, 5:17). In the book of Acts, the Spirit enables Peter to preach the most powerful sermon of his life, and empowers the disciples to speak in different languages so the good news of Jesus could be shared with many more people. The book of Romans says that the Spirit of God raised Jesus from the dead (Romans 8:11).

Now in our text, the Spirit of God gives spiritual gifts, and energizes and guides their use. For me, this is freeing and applies also to the gift of creativity. It's a gift that's freely given—we don't have to earn it or compete for it. We don't have to drive ourselves. We don't have to be guilted into doing anything. Whatever creative gifts we may have, we receive them from God, whose Spirit leads and enables us to express them.

INTEGRATING

1. **In *The Artist's Rule*,** Christine Valters Paintner explores creativity and spirituality, art and spiritual practice, embracing and integrating both our "spiritual path and creative longings" (p. 1). How are prayer and spiritual practice part of your creative life? In what ways does the Spirit guide your creative process?

2 . Human imagination is a gift from God, but it can also be used in unhealthy and destructive ways. In Scripture, people have sometimes imagined idols (Exodus 32:1-4; Isaiah 44:9-20) or used their creativity to "devise violence" (Proverbs 24:1-2) or "devise evil" (Zechariah 7:8-10). How might we guard our imaginations and use them in healthy ways?

3 . At Jesus' baptism, the Holy Spirit appears like a dove (Matthew 3:16; Mark 1:10; Luke 3:22; John 1:32). Try your hand at folding paper doves using traditional origami by finding instructions on the Internet or in other resources. It's okay if your dove doesn't turn out exactly like you think it should—just have fun with it, and enjoy the colors and feel of the paper.

SENDING

- Sing "There Are Many Gifts" (*Hymnal: A Worship Book* #304) or "Come, O Spirit, Come" (*Sing the Story* #104).

- Pray for God's Spirit of peace wherever there is trouble:
    Holy Spirit, we acknowledge your unseen and inspiring presence.
    Energize and enable our creativity to serve you and others. Amen.

ten . . . .

1 Corinthians 10:31; 15:58; Ephesians 6:7; Colossians 3:17

For creative success, the most important audience is the audience of One

OVERVIEW

One day I made a batch of my mother's famous chocolate chip cookies for a youth meeting. "These are so good, you should make these every day!" said one youth as he reached for his third cookie. "With that kind of appreciation, maybe I should," I thought to myself. What a treat to be met with such enthusiasm!

Not every creative endeavor gets that kind of response, of course. At times, others may be indifferent or may offer a lukewarm response. We may face outright rejection of a creative vision that we believe is God-given. We may look around and wonder why it's always someone else who has written the bestseller, someone else who has just won another quilting award, someone else who can run faster or solve problems more quickly. From my own experience, I know that making such comparisons or placing too much weight on the opinions of others leads inevitably to discouragement and feelings of failure. In this session we explore another way.

VISUAL

A large candle

GATHERING

Light the candle, and read the following litany:

One: O God and Creator of all, gather us into your presence.

All: *We confess that we are often distracted by the many voices in our world and by our own noisy spirits. Focus our attention now to be present to you.*

One: Dear Jesus, Emmanuel, God-with-us, be our teacher.

All: *We have much to learn to be gentle and humble in heart, to rest ourselves in you. Teach us to listen for your voice.*

One: Holy Spirit, guide and inspiration, direct our path.

All: *We seek clarity of vision and courage for the way. Enable us to praise and serve the Lord. Amen.*

DEEPENING

The ancient city of Corinth sprawled across a narrow bridge of land that connected the mainland with a large peninsula. The city controlled land access between the two, and boasted two seaports, one on either side of the city. Its position as a hub for major land and waterways made it a center for commerce and industry.

In this busy urban setting, the church of Corinth included a diverse group of people with a lively faith and many spiritual gifts. But the very richness and strength of their diversity had a shadow side. Instead of seeking to encourage one another, different groups within the church stood in opposition, claiming to follow Paul or Apollos, Cephas or Christ, with each group claiming to be better than the others. The church became divided over issues of sexuality, what to do about eating meat sacrificed to idols, and other controversies.

In this situation of conflict, the apostle Paul reminded the Corinthians of the work of Christ (1 Corinthians 1:18ff.). If they were going to boast at all, they should boast in what Christ had accomplished for them by his suffering and death (v. 31). From this common foundation of faith and unity in Christ, Paul goes on to address the controversies among them, writing at length about freedom, self-discipline, and church discipline. In the course of his discussion, he sums up his teaching, "So, whether you eat or drink, or whatever you do, do everything for the glory of God" (10:31). Near the end of his letter, he encourages them, "Therefore, my beloved, be steadfast, immovable, always excelling in the work of the Lord, because you know that in the Lord your labor is not in vain" (15:58).

This focus on serving God is not unique to Paul's letter to the Corinthians. Ephesians 6:7 says, "Render service with enthusiasm, as to the Lord and not to men and women," and Colossians 3:17: "And whatever you do, in word or deed, do everything in the name of the Lord Jesus, giving thanks to God the Father through him." In Paul's view, God is the main audience for the Corinthians, for the whole church, and I'm sure he would affirm that for us today. Our creative efforts are part of the "everything" that Paul addresses, so we might well paraphrase his teaching: whatever you do with your creativity, do it for God's glory—excel in it not out of pride or for financial gain, but because you serve the Lord.

INTEGRATING

1. What does it mean for you to excel at expressing your creativity? How is it the same as, or different from, excelling "in the work of the Lord"? Do you ever experience a conflict between creative excellence and being faithful to God's work in your life?

2. Humanly speaking, who is the audience for your creative efforts? What have you learned from those who have expressed appreciation for what you do? What have you learned from your critics? How do you avoid falling into the trap of comparing yourself with others?

3. Sing "Let the Whole Creation Cry" (*Hymnal: A Worship Book* #51), and find creative ways to make music together; for example, invite musicians to play along; add a joyful noise with simple percussion instruments such as bells, wood blocks, tambourines, and so forth; divide the group in two and alternate singing the main lines ("Let the whole creation cry"; "Glory to the Lord on high"; and so on), with everyone joining in on the "Alleluias." Name the different parts of creation in this hymn. What does their participation say about God as the source and audience of creativity?

SENDING

- Sing "Jesus, Be the Center" (*Sing the Story* #31) and/or "Be Thou My Vision" (*Hymnal: A Worship Book* #545).

- Close with this 16th-century prayer for God's presence:
    God be in my head, and in my understanding;
    God be in mine eyes, and in my looking;
    God be in my mouth, and in my speaking;
    God be in my heart, and in my thinking;
    God be at mine end, and at my departing.
    (*Extinguish the candle and depart in peace.*)

eleven . . . .

Philippians 4:4-9

"Creativity is a way of living life."
—MADELEINE L'ENGLE

OVERVIEW

I've always thought of creating as "making something," so I was surprised to discover that historically the most basic meaning of *create* is simply to "grow" (from the Proto-Indo-European root word *kerh*). As growth unfolds as a natural part of life even before birth, so creativity unfolds and blossoms as part of life too. In the words of Madeleine L'Engle, "Creativity is a way of living life, no matter our vocation or how we earn our living. Creativity is not limited to the arts, or having some kind of important career" (*Walking on Water*, p. 90).

To experience creativity as part of daily living, it helps to slow down and pay attention: to slow down and savor the taste and texture of the food we eat, to slow down and notice the colors around us, to slow down and be deliberate about the way we arrange our lives, to slow down and allow God to teach us and grow us. In this session, we slow down to experience Scripture.

VISUAL

An item of beauty

GATHERING

The church of Philippi was in distress, with their church planter arrested and imprisoned because of his faith in Jesus (Philippians 1:12-14). Other preachers had arrived to stir up trouble (1:17). Believers were suffering (1:29), and two of their members were in conflict (4:2-3). Yet for all these troubles, the letter to the Philippians bubbles with joy: "constantly praying with joy" (1:4), "I will continue to rejoice" (1:18), "rejoice with me" (2:18), "my joy and crown" (4:1), "Rejoice in the Lord always; again I will say, Rejoice." (4:4).

Just as the Philippians experienced joy even in the midst of difficulty, living with creativity and joy today does not depend on our circumstances. Having a room of one's own, being well rested and in a beautiful setting with supportive relationships may be ideal, but creativity can take root and grow anywhere—in songs born of heartache, with children fashioning musical instruments from garbage (see #2 in *Integrating*), in the development of alternative energy sources, and in other creative problem solving.

DEEPENING

In my book *Sacred Pauses: Spiritual Practices for Personal Renewal*, I describe *lectio divina* as a way of praying Scripture. Instead of reading Scripture primarily for information or instruction, in *lectio divina* I listen for the Spirit in the words of Scripture. Instead of praying primarily to tell God what I want, in *lectio divina* I listen for what God is telling me.

One of the beauties of this practice is that a year from now, a week from now, even tomorrow, God may use the same text to speak to me in a different way. In group settings, I've noticed that different people may hear God speak in different ways even though we hear the same words read in the same way at the same time. *Lectio divina* seems to open up new possibilities—dare I say creative possibilities—for God to speak to us.

In its simplest form, *lectio divina* is simply paying attention to Scripture. As you read or listen to the text, where does God draw your attention? Read or listen a second time, and notice where your attention rests. Stay with that particular word or phrase, and experience the text again. What is God saying to you, and how does this apply to your own situation?

In my own *lectio divina* on this text, I find myself drawn to "do not be anxious about anything." A colleague and his family grieve the death of their son, and I am preparing for the funeral. *Do not be anxious about anything.* A dear church member is now in palliative care in the hospital. *Do not be anxious about anything.* I have writing deadlines looming and a sermon to finish for Sunday. *Do not be anxious about anything.* We're out of bread and fresh fruit, and I need to get to the store before it closes. *Do not be anxious about anything.*

As I sit quietly with these words, I sense God's Spirit surrounding me and wrapping me in a blanket of peace. Some might say it's my overactive imagination, or the product of too few hours of sleep last night, but I believe that "the peace of God, which surpasses all understanding" guards my heart and mind. Thank you, God, for your reassuring presence.

Try your own *lectio divina* with Philippians 4:4-9. Begin with slowing down. Sit comfortably, breathe deeply, quiet your spirit, and listen for God's Spirit. Read or listen to the text. What word or phrase draws your attention? What is God saying to you?

INTEGRATING

1. Reread Philippians 4:8, and choose one of the key words. Write your one word on a piece of paper, then use colored pencils or markers to embellish, doodle, and draw around it. What color seems to illustrate your word best? Does it lend itself to straight lines, circles, or other shapes? What questions does your word raise for you?

2. Do an Internet search for a video about *Landfill Harmonic*. What does it communicate about art, beauty, creativity, and community? What creative possibilities does it open up for you?

3. Brainstorm ideas for more creative living, and choose one or more to practice this week. Here are a few ideas to get you started: try a new food, add a pop of color to what you normally wear, daydream, carry a notebook to jot down ideas. Add as many other ideas as you can to this list.

SENDING

- Read Ephesians 3:20 from *The Message*: "God can do anything, you know—far more than you could ever imagine or guess or request in your wildest dreams! He does it not by pushing us around but by working within us, his Spirit deeply and gently within us."

- Sing "Take My Life" (*Hymnal: A Worship Book* #389).

- Pass the peace by saying: "The God of peace will be with you" (Philippians 4:9).

twelve . . . .

2 Timothy 1:1-14

Fan into flame the spark within you

OVERVIEW

As a young church leader, Timothy exercised his gifts in worship, preaching, and teaching. He accompanied Paul on his second missionary journey, and later travelled on Paul's behalf to encourage churches in Corinth and Thessalonica. In 1 Timothy 4:14, Paul encourages him, "Do not neglect the gift that is in you," and says much the same again in 2 Timothy 1:6: "rekindle the gift of God that is within you." Even as he exercised his gifts, Timothy was still growing into them and benefited from Paul's encouragement and mentoring.

What does it take to nurture and grow our creative gifts? Young and old, men and women, leaders and preachers, computer programmers and cooks, listeners and musicians—whatever our gifts and roles, we can neglect and bury them as one fearful servant tried to do, or we can celebrate and practice them in ways that allow those sparks to grow and flourish. In this session, we reflect on the kindling and rekindling of Timothy's gifts and what we can learn for our own creativity today.

VISUAL

A tealight for each woman

GATHERING

As in most of his letters, Paul begins 2 Timothy with a brief saluta-tion and blessing (1:1-2), followed by prayer and thanksgiving to God (vv. 3-5). In the body of the letter, he reviews his own situa-tion of imprisonment and suffering, his calling as an apostle and teacher (vv. 8-12), and encourages Timothy to follow his example (vv. 8, 13). In all of this, he reassures Timothy of the Holy Spirit's gift, presence, and help (vv. 6-7, 14).

Sing the old gospel hymn "I Know Not Why God's Wondrous" (*Hymnal: A Worship Book* #338) as a gathering song. Note how the first line concludes, "I *know not* why God's wondrous grace to me he hath made *known*" (emphasis added). The interplay of known and unknown continue throughout the hymn: I know not why, how, or when at the beginning of each verse, and the ringing affir-mation of the refrain, "But I know whom I have believed." Unseen and mysteriously, the Spirit is at work "creating faith" (verse 3).

DEEPENING

As I read Timothy's story, I'm amazed at the Spirit's work in his life, preparing and enabling him as a leader. From Paul's letter, it's clear that Timothy had a legacy of faith from his mother, Eunice, and his grandmother, Lois. He had an experienced mentor in Paul, who prayed for him, encouraged him, and entrusted him with responsibilities in the church. With these close personal rela-tionships, the Spirit formed a circle of support around Timothy's ministry and leadership.

While Timothy was a gifted leader with a good support system, the text seems to suggest that he also needed a boost of self-confidence. At least, Paul makes a point of reminding him that "God did not give us a spirit of cowardice" (v. 7) and "do not be ashamed" (v. 8). Instead, Paul reminds Timothy that God had given him "a spirit of power and of love, and self-discipline" (v. 7).

The word *power* here is the Greek *dunamis*, which is the ability to get things done. It's the root of our English word *dynamite*. But in this case, the power is not out of control and destructive. It's tempered by love—the Greek *agape*, which is the love God extends to us and we reflect back to God and to our neighbor—and by self-discipline—the Greek *sophronismo*, which is sound-minded and prudent. So the ability to get things done is also restrained by love and directed by self-discipline.

So too with creativity. There is a time just to get things done— to write that impossibly messy and unwieldy first draft—then to prune it back with love and self-discipline to give it form and focus. It's empowering to take photograph after photograph after photograph, and then an exercise in good judgement to choose just the right ones to make into fabulous greeting cards to give away with love.

In one study, researchers took a group of children to a playground that didn't have a fence, and they observed that the children played mainly in the middle area. Then they took the children to another playground that was approximately the same, only the second playground had a fence around it. This time, they discovered that the children used all of the playground right up to the fence. Having the fence as a boundary actually gave them more freedom and enabled them to be more creative with the entire area. In our creative life, having boundaries in the form of self-control can also be freeing.

INTEGRATING

1. Which spirit from God do you most claim in owning your creativity—the spirit of power, of love, or of self-discipline? Which one is the most difficult for you to claim?

2. In what ways are you a mentor in creativity? What art or skill have you passed on, or would like to pass on, to your children and grandchildren, or another younger person? Who can you encourage?

3. Do an Internet search for Scripture doodle art. Have colored pencils and markers available for women to choose a Bible verse and do their own artistic reflection and doodle art.

SENDING

- Invite each woman to make her own affirmation: "God has given me a spirit of power, love, and self-discipline in expressing my creativity," and then to light one of the tealights.

- Sing "This Little Light of Mine" (*Hymnal: A Worship Book* #401).

- Stand in a circle and invite the women to set their tealights on the floor in front of them. Lay hands on one another by placing your hands on the shoulders of those on either side of you. Offer one another the blessing based on 2 Timothy 1:2: "You are God's beloved child: Grace, mercy, and peace from God the Father and Christ Jesus our Lord."

- Extinguish the tealights, and have each woman take her tealight home.

Psalm 148

Closing Worship: Creativity Continues

VISUAL

Decorate a bulletin board and have pins available to post creativity statements during the offering time. You could also use poster board and tape if a bulletin board is not available.

Place visuals from previous sessions around the room as a reminder of your exploration of creativity.

GATHERING

Sing one or more of the following suggested songs.
Hymnal: A Worship Book
   #6 Here In This Place
   #26 Holy Spirit, Come With Power
   #70 Immortal, Invisible, God Only Wise
Sing the Story
   #122 Let All Creation Dance

Although our study of creativity now draws to a close with this worship celebration, our creativity is meant to continue and flourish. How has your spark of creativity been ignited in these sessions? What have you learned? How will you continue to express your creativity? Take some time for personal reflection and sharing on these questions before continuing in worship.

PRAISING

Read Psalm 148.

PROCLAIMING

Ask five women to read the following list, with each woman reading 10 of the creativity statements.

Fifty ways to be (more) creative.
1. Go for a nature walk.
2. Hum as you wash dishes by hand.
3. Worship in a setting different from your own.
4. Write new words to an old hymn tune.
5. Start a daily prayer practice.
6. Plant bulbs.
7. Visit an art gallery.
8. Walk a labyrinth.
9. Paint a room.
10. Plant a tree.
11. Look at the sky.
12. Find a mentor for your creative efforts.
13. Sew gift bags instead of using wrapping paper.
14. Braid your hair.
15. Invite someone new to supper.
16. Write a poem.
17. Spend 10 minutes daydreaming with God.
18. Write a story about how you got your name.
19. Try a new flavor of ice cream.
20. Plan a family activity or outing.

21. Read a classic novel.
22. Make your own Christmas decorations.
23. Write an encouraging note to someone who needs to be cheered up.
24. Color with a child.
25. Whistle.
26. Crochet or knit a scarf.
27. Walk, bike, or take public transit.
28. Go on a pilgrimage.
29. Build a model airplane.
30. Do a jigsaw puzzle.
31. Do a random act of kindness.
32. Go to the library.
33. Talk to your plants.
34. Bake a pie (or cookies) to bring to your neighbors.
35. Experiment with a new recipe.
36. Collaborate on a project.
37. Learn another language.
38. Come up with a new knock-knock joke.
39. Write and mail a letter to a friend.
40. Arrange flowers.
41. Play the piano as a joyful noise to the Lord.
42. Draw a self-portrait.
43. Go to bed early.
44. Stay up late.
45. Teach someone a skill.
46. Make a slide show set to music.
47. Join a choir.
48. Grow vegetables.
49. Spend a day with your kids outdoors.
50. Participate in a Taizé service.

OFFERING

Pass out index cards and invite each woman to write one or more creativity statements of her own. These could be adapted from the reading, statements directly related to her own art or skill, or an activity or insight from this series. Invite women to speak these as well, and to add their statements to the bulletin board.

PRAYING

Dedicate the creativity statements that have been offered.

Read the prayer "Bless the Work of Our Hands, O God."

> Bless the work of our hands, O God.
>
> Bless the hands that move earth, plant seeds and harvest,
> hands with calluses and dirty fingernails, strong hands.
>
> Bless the hands that drive cars and trucks and forklifts,
> hands that spend time on computer keyboards, capable hands.
>
> Bless the hands that manufacture and create,
> working wood and metal and plastic, practical hands.
>
> Bless the hands that wash, mop and scrub,
> hands that know what to do with soap, determined hands.
>
> Bless the hands that play instruments and hold paintbrushes,
> hands that are creative tools, artistic hands.
>
> Bless the hands that cook and feed, heal and nurture,
> hands with a gentle touch, loving hands.

Bless the hands that give away money or food,
hands that are always trying to be empty, Christ-like hands.

Our hands do the work of your hands, O God our Creator.
Amen.[1]

SENDING

Leave the bulletin board and creativity statements on display over the next weeks, if possible; if not, invite each woman to take several statements to post somewhere at home.

Suggested Songs
Hymnal: A Worship Book
#429 Go Now In Peace
#434 Thuma Mina
Sing the Journey
#56 Make Me a Channel of Your Peace
Sing the Story
#121 Nothing Is Lost on the Breath of God

Benediction

And now may the wind of the Spirit continue to inspire you,

may Jesus walk with you from one creative step to the next,

may God the Creator enliven and encourage you

today and every day. Amen.

---

1. Carol Penner, used by permission, www.leadinginworship.com

Resources

Bayles, David, and Ted Orland. *Art and Fear: Observations on the Rewards (and Perils) of Artmaking*. Santa Cruz, CA: Image Continuum, 1993.

Elliot, Jeffrey M. *Conversations with Maya Angelou*. Jackson: University Press of Mississippi, 1989.

Hymnal: A Worship Book. Newton, KS: Faith & Life Press, 1992.

L'Engle, Madeleine. *Walking on Water: Reflections on Faith and Art*. Wheaton, IL: Harold Shaw Publishers, 1980.

Luther, Martin. Preface to the Revised Edition of the *German Psalter*, 1531. http://www.cprf.co.uk/quotes /martinlutherpsalter.htm#.VGqcIfnF9-c.

Mann, Douglas C. *The Art of Helping Others: How Artists Can Serve God and Love the World*. Downers Grove, IL: IVP Books, 2014.

Paintner, Christine Valters. *The Artist's Rule: Nurturing Your Creative Soul with Monastic Wisdom*. Notre Dame, IN: Sorin Books, 2011.

Peterson, Eugene H. *The Message Remix: The Bible in Contemporary Language*. Colorado Springs, CO: NavPress, 2003.

Rookmaker, Hans. *The Creative Gift*. Westchester, IL: Cornerstone Books, 1981.

Shine On: A Story Bible. Harrisonburg, VA: MennoMedia, 2014.

Sing the Journey. Newton, KS: Faith & Life Resources, 2005.

Sing the Story. Newton, KS: Faith & Life Resources, 2007.

Van Gogh, Vincent. Letter to Theo Van Gogh. Arles, France, September 17, 1888. http://www.webexhibits.org/vangogh /letter/18/538.htm.

Yamasaki, April. *Sacred Pauses: Spiritual Practices for Personal Renewal.* Harrisonburg, VA: Herald Press, 2013.

About Mennonite Women Canada

As each has received a gift, employ it for one another, as good stewards of God's varied grace. —1 Peter 4:10

Mission statement

Mennonite Women Canada encourages women to:

- nurture their life in Christ
- acknowledge and share their gifts
- hear and support each other
- serve and minister across the street and around the world

We commit ourselves to:

- Promote spiritual growth through Bible study, prayer, and fellowship.
- Discern and nurture women's gifts and skills for leadership and service in the local church, the community, and the world.
- Build relationships and networks for support, affirmation, discernment, witness, service, and celebration.
- Support and strengthen the missional outreach of Mennonite Church Canada.

We do this through:

- Publication of an annual Bible Study Guide partnering with Mennonite Women USA.

- Providing scholarships for women studying Anabaptist theology at a master's level through our Spiritual Growth Assistance Fund.

- Connecting women across Canada via our semiannual newsletter, *Connections*, and bimonthly pages in the *Canadian Mennonite* magazine under the headline "Women Walking Together in Faith."

- Supporting and encouraging women working in Mennonite Church Canada's ministries through our Pennies and Prayer Legacy Fund.

- Maintaining a web page at http://women.mennonitechurch .ca/ and a blog at http://mennowomencanada.blogspot.com/.

- Connecting with and supporting the provincial/area women's organizations through our executive meetings in March and at Mennonite Church Canada Assembly sessions.

We as Mennonite Women Canada are striving to do God's will and work where we are to the best of our ability. You too can be a part!

More information is available at our website (see address above).
Connect with us on our blog (see address above).
Contact the president at presmwcanada@mennonitechurch.ca
or write to
Mennonite Women Canada c/o Mennonite Church Canada
600 Shaftesbury Blvd., Winnipeg, MB R3P 0M4

About Mennonite Women USA

Jesus said: "I am the vine. You are the branches." —John 15:5

Mission Statement

Our mission at Mennonite Women USA is to empower women and women's groups as we nurture our life in Christ through studying the Bible, using our gifts, hearing each other, and engaging in mission and service.

Our Vision: Mennonite Women USA invites women across generations, cultures, and places to share and honor our stories, care for each other, and express our prophetic voice boldly as we seek to follow Christ.

In living our mission, Mennonite Women USA:

- Connects globally by funding scholarships for women worldwide for church leadership training through our International Women's Fund.

- Provides Sister Care seminars giving women tools for ongoing personal healing, for recognizing and celebrating God's grace in their lives, and for responding more confidently and effectively to the needs of others in their families, congregations, and communities. Sister Care seminars have been shared throughout North America and internationally as a leadership training resource.

- Resources women's groups across the United States through leadership training and by sponsoring an annual Anabaptist Bible study guide written by and for women.

- Fosters relationships through the Sister-Link program emphasizing mutual giving and receiving and validating a wide variety of gifts.

- Speaks prophetically by sharing stories of women of all ages and backgrounds through *Timbrel* magazine, the publication of Mennonite Women USA. *Timbrel* is published quarterly and is also available as an online publication.

We'd love to tell you more about our ministry.

Learn more about Mennonite Women USA programs—and get a little lift in your day—by signing up for our free monthly e-letter, "A Postcard & a Prayer." Just send us your name, address, and email to the address below.

More information is available at: www.MWUSA.org.
Mennonite Women USA
718 N. Main St.
Newton, KS 67114-1819
316.281.4396 or 866.866.2872, ext. 34396
office@MennoniteWomenUSA.org

About the Writer

April Yamasaki is lead pastor of Emmanuel Mennonite Church in Abbotsford, British Columbia. She loves the big picture of focusing the church on following Jesus, being community-minded, and having a global perspective. She is a catalyst and encourager to engage people in using their gifts, and enjoys expressing her love of Scripture and creativity in worship and preaching.

Beyond her pastoral work, April blogs on writing and other acts of faith. She has published numerous articles and several books, most recently *Sacred Pauses: Spiritual Practices for Personal Renewal* (Herald Press) and *Ordinary Time with Jesus* (CSS Publishing). Other publications include *Remember Lot's Wife and Other Unnamed Women of the Bible* (faithQuest), *Making Disciples: A Manual for Baptism and Church Membership* (Faith & Life Press), and a collaboration with photographer Lois Siemens, entitled *my Sacred Pauses daybook 2015* (Loishelen Designs).

April has a bachelor of arts (University of British Columbia) and a master's degree in Christian studies (Regent College). She has taught college-level courses in Bible and English, adult continuing education courses on spiritual practices, and seminars and retreats on faith, work, rest, and Christian living.

A third-generation Canadian of Chinese descent, April was born and raised in Vancouver, British Columbia, and has lived on the campuses of Anabaptist Mennonite Biblical Seminary in Elkhart, Indiana, and Union Presbyterian Seminary in Richmond,

Virginia. She lives in Abbotsford with her husband, Gary, who teaches biblical studies at Columbia Bible College.

Visit her website at www.aprilyamasaki.com.